TWELVE-STEP WORKBOOK
STEP FIVE SIX AND SEVEN
INTO ACTION

A companion workbook series to Butterflies and Paratroopers Are Not Born with Wings:
A Warrior's Guide to BeingHappy, Joyous, and Free
Available on AMAZON.COM and at BPBOOKS.NET

MILO

© 2022 B&P BookWorks, LLC
Twelve Step Workbook- Big Book Study is a companion workbook series to the primary textbook **Butterflies and Paratroopers Are Not Born with Wings: A Warrior's Guide to Being Happy, Joyous, and Free.** All rights reserved. No part of this book may be reproduced in whole or in part, stored in a retrieval system, or transmitted in any form, or by any means, electronic, mechanical, photocopying, recording, or otherwise, without prior permission of B&P BookWorks, LLC.

Note To Reader

This workbook is part of the series Twelve Step Workbook. In this series, each step is broken down to provide the directions on how to the step as written in the book Alcoholics Anonymous. A table outlining the Big Book Step Study Format can be found on page 6 of this workbook.

These workbooks are also a companion series to the author's primary work, *Butterflies and Paratroopers Are Not Born With Wings: A Warrior Guide to Being Happy, Joyous, and Free.* In that book, Milo trains a butterfly to become a paratrooper. That's not easy. Neither is recovery from alcohol, drugs, food, people, or whatever.

Butterflies and Paratroopers is not a regurgitated recovery book. First, it's funny. Second, it's one-of-a-kind. Third, it's not a self-help book. It's an operator's manual for alcoholics, drug addicts, codependents, overeaters, and whoever else has an addictive personality with a smidge of OCD or a dusting of ADHD.

With a lighthearted iron fist in a velvet glove *Butterflies and Paratroopers* is written in the persona of an Army First Sergeant. With wit and sarcasm, Milo lays out the clear-cut simple directions to operate the most complex, out-of-warranty, prone to breakdown piece of equipment ever made—that's you.

Using amusing "sober snippets" and "recovery war stories", Milo connects real-life trials, tribulations, pandemonium, and predicaments, with spirituality, sobriety, sanity, and serenity. You'll quickly see the similarities between the army and twelve-step recovery programs. Both take anyone who walks through the door and has a wrench to fit any nut that does.

As *Butterflies and Paratroopers,* and this series, relies heavily on the Big Book, reprint permission was sought and received from Alcoholics Anonymous World Services, Inc. Office of Intellectual Property before publication. While excerpts, in whole or part herein, are reprinted with permission of Alcoholics Anonymous World Services, Inc. it neither approves nor necessarily agrees with the views expressed. A.A. is a program of recovery for alcoholism only. Use of the Twelve Steps in connection with programs and activities which are patterned after A.A., but which address other problems, or in any other non-A.A. context, does not imply otherwise.

Contents

Five: Forgiveness 4

Six and Seven: Humility 10

12 and 12 Step Five 24

12 and 12 Step 6 30

12 and 12 Step Seven 36

Steps Five, Six and Seven Closeout 40

Big Book Step Study Format 42

Butterflies and Paratroopers Are Not Born With Wings 43

About the Author 44

Answers 45

Five: Forgiveness

We know you are weary from carrying us on your back. We would do anything to help relieve you of this burden except of course, get off your back. (Tolstoy)

The most critical part of an airborne operation is not the jumping, but the landing. To get in the fight, one must land uninjured. Step Five is like a Parachute Landing Fall (PLF). It gets you on your feet and into the fight. Being airborne is not about getting ready; it's about going on order. Paratroopers have a saying: "If we can't carry it, we don't need it." So, they unload what's not needed and move out onto the firing line of life. If you are a one-pound bag filled with ten pounds of trash, it's time to take it all to the dumpster.

Completing Step Four, you think you've been knocked down. Yet, it's only the first round. It's capitulation, but not surrender. You're giving in, not giving up. It's in the fifth you get back on your feet. In the paratroopers, if you can still fight, you're not a casualty. And, since this is a life-and-death errand, we can waste no time, for again, faith without works is dead.

In the Lord's Prayer, we ask for forgiveness. It's auto granted, but with a catch. It's that pesky "forgive those who have trespassed against us" clause. This will be the fight of your life that saves your life.

"Wait, what? Didn't we take care of this when we wrote all those transgressions against us? And now you want us to forgive them too? What's that about?" Here's the how and why of it. Step Five is a new mission. It's neither punishment, confession, nor inquisition. We can waste no time. It's time to get it all off our chest to get them all off our backs. No need to hold anything back. God knows what you've done. He's forgiven you. Now it's your turn to learn how to forgive others. And in so doing, we begin to learn how to forgive ourself. Which is what this work is all about.

A fifth is larger than a pint but smaller than a quart. Drinking nips means you need to keep going back for more. Trying to dump the wreckage of your past in bits and pieces sets you up for holding on to the worst items in stock. As mom said, it hurts less to rip the bandage off the boo-boo all at once. An infectious malady requires a spiritual remedy. For when the spiritual malady is overcome, only than do we straighten out mentally and physically. Step Five is essential in overcoming a spiritual malady. "If we skip this vital step, we may not overcome drinking."

A new chapter of life starts with Step Five. Our newfound willingness is up against self-centered power, prestige, and property. There is a constant tension between humiliation and hubris, and humility and humanity. Finding that needle in the haystack to repair the fabric of your existence is not a job for Goldilocks. It's a job for God.

1. The most critical part of an airborne operation is _____ _____.

2. Step Five gets _____ _____ _____ _____ and into the fight.

3. Completing the inventory is only the _____

4. Being on a _____ and _____ _____ we can waste no time.

5. True or False? In the Lord's Prayer, the forgiveness we ask for granted

6. In receiving forgiveness from God there is a catch.

7. What is that pesky catch?

8. True or False? Step Five is punishment, a confession, and an inquisition.

9. In learning how to forgive others, _____ _____ to learn how to forgive ourself. '

10. True or False? Which is what this work is all about.

11. Trying to dump the wreckage of your past in bits and pieces sets you up for holding on to the _____ _____ _____ _____.

12. To straighten out mentally and physically we must first straighten out _____.

13. If we skip the fifth step what may happen?

If you think Step Five won't work for you, that's alcoholism. Most who go to AA attempt a Fourth and Fifth Step. Some start, then stop, then pick it up again. Some make no effort at all. You don't need to do this work to stay white-knuckled sober. Four and five is the basic training for ten and eleven. You'll need this training "as you trudge the Road of Happy Destiny."

If Catholic, your first Fifth Step is at age seven. It's called Confession. Scared shitless, you make up things you didn't do and leave out the things you did. Yes, Catholics lie in Confession. We'll leave out anything to get away with a penance of one Our Father, three Hail Mary, and a Glory Be. This lying to get away with it is a pattern that continues from then until we complete the seventh step.

Step Five is not a cure, it's a diagnosis. Its purpose is to develop a new attitude and a new relationship with your Creator. It's not for shaming, blaming, or complaining. It's for identifying and being free of what is holding us back. This makes the fifth about looking forward, not back. As said, it's not a confession, but rather an admission of the repetitive and trivial practices that have ruled our life. It is upon this admission we receive absolution.

Freedom of the bondage of self follows forgiveness. It can't proceed it. And forgiveness is the price you must pay for that freedom. It's a steep price. For if you give something away, and it costs you nothing, then what's it worth? You better understand what it means to forgive others before you do it. Remember a harpoon hurts a lot more coming out then going in.

First, it's not a two-way street. When most people say, "forget it," even if they mean it, they don't forget it. Second, it's expensive. In granting clemency, you give up being a victim. You can't bitch about it anymore. Third, it's non-refundable. Forgiveness is not a commodity we barter for. Its value comes from being given freely, and forever. Fourth, it's not transferable. You don't get to forgive people for what they didn't do. And as important, you don't forgive yourself for what someone else did. Fifth, granting forgiveness is the greatest gift you will ever give yourself.

In a Thucydides Trap, pride and fear come as a pair. They are the bookends that hold in place the barriers to truth. Forgiveness is the act of pocketing pride and overcoming fear. It's the Fifth Step that sucks the truth out of you.

With the alcoholic, drug addict, codependent, overeater, whatever (ADCOW) the solution is always more. They are right. Addiction to God for relief is the answer. And since nature abhors a vacuum, you best be careful what gets sucked back inside of you. It best be more of God, and less of you. That's why the Steps are in a specific sequence for a reason. In the fifth step we are not concerned with setting things right. Insha'Allah, we'll do that later. What we are concerned about is getting rid of those people riding on our back and squatting in our head.

1. If you think Step Five won't work for you, _____ _____.

2. True or False? Most who go to AA attempt a Fourth and Fifth Step.

3. True or False? Step Four and Five have nothing to do with the rest of the steps.

4. With the alcoholic lying to get away with something is a pattern that continues until we _____ _____ _____ _____.

5. Step Five is not a cure, but a _____.

6. True or False? Step Five is for shaming, blaming, or complaining.

7. True or False? The fifth step is about looking forward, not back.

8. The fifth step is rather an admission of the _____ and _____ practices that have ruled our life.

9. It is upon this _____ we receive _____..

10. Forgiveness is?
    - Not a two-way street
    - Expensive.
    - Non-refundable
    - Non-transferrable
    - Best gift of all
    - All the above

11. Forgiveness is the act of _____ _____ and _____ _____.

12. The Fifth Step that sucks the _____ _____ _____ _____..

13. True or False? In the fifth step we are not concerned with setting things right.

Sunlight is the best disinfectant. Sewage treatment is a physical, biological, and chemical procedure. It's the turbidity you harbor that clouds your thoughts and cuts you off from the Sunlight of the Spirit. Going through a sequential and defined process changes an odorous influent into a clear effluent.

The Fifth Step works like a sewage treatment plant: it cleans up the shit from your past. It turns calamity into serenity. Think about this step as flushing the toilet. So, if you're an alcoholic who has done this work, don't let any erudite say, "You don't know shit." Doesn't it make you happy when people know you are right?

Step Five is more than admitting to God, ourselves, and another person. It's becoming aware of the exact nature of our defects (note change in word). We know discussing our defects is difficult. Wasn't admitting them to ourselves adequate? Why isn't a solitary self-appraisal sufficient? Why will we be more reconciled, discussing ourselves with another person? Because the lies we tell ourselves, are the hardest to disprove. The mechanics of Step Five means enduring an experience we are not accustomed to. That would be telling the truth.

We alcoholics are quite the performers. Our Shakespearean wo-is-me moments are as convincing as the "I am the greatest" one. Only the latter is fleeting and soon lost. As the book says," We want to enjoy a reputation we know in our heart we don't deserve." Still, we push-on with just don't drink, go to meetings, and tell anyone who will listen about the people, places, and things that are pissing us off. Having persevered with the don't drink, go to meetings, and ask for help strategy, how than is relapse possible? Could it be they start their inventory but hold on to their "worst items in stock"? Or, could it be, they never complete their housecleaning? Is this because pride and fear prevent them from heeding the warning, we find it necessary to tell someone *all* our life story?

Inviting God into the process we pocket our pride, overcome fear, and are able to withhold nothing. We disclose "every dark cranny of the past." When finished, we are delighted. The Big Book says, "We can look the world in the eye. We are at peace and ease. Our fears fall from us. We feel a new nearness to our creator. Until now, we had certain spiritual beliefs, but now we begin to have a spiritual experience."

What's next?
- We return home and sit quietly for an hour.
- We thank God from the bottom of our hearts that we got to know Him better.
- We take our book down off the shelf.
- Opening it to the Twelve Steps, we review the first five proposals.

1. What is the best disinfectant?

2. The turbidity you harbor clouds cuts you off from the _____ ____ ____ _____.

3. Going through a sequential process (the steps) changes an _____ _____ into a clear effluent.

4. We can think about the fifth step as _____ _____ _____.

5. What makes an alcoholic happy?

6. True or False? Step Five is more than admitting to God, ourselves, and another person.

7. Why isn't a solitary self-appraisal sufficient?

8. What is the word change in step five after completing four?

9. The mechanics of Step Five means enduring what experience we are not accustomed to?

10. Having persevered with the don't drink, go to meetings, and ask for help strategy, how is relapse possible?

11. By inviting God into the process, we pocket our _____, overcome _____, and withhold _____.

12. When finished with reading our inventory what's next?
    A. We return home and sit quietly for an hour.
    B. We thank God from the bottom of our hearts that we got to know Him better.
    C. We take our book down off the shelf.
    D. Opening it to the Twelve Steps, we review the first five proposals.
    E. All the above
    F. None of the above

Once assured that we have been thorough and honest in taking inventory and that our long talk was calm, frank and open we are ready to conclude this step. How do we do that? We take the Fifth Step final exam.
- Is our work solid so far?
- Are the stones properly in place?
- Have we skipped on the cement?
- Have we tried to make mortar without sand?
- Have we omitted anything?

If you have been thorough and honest, written down a lot, and had a long talk, you will pass this exam. It is here you exit your past life. Passing through a metaphysical arch receiving freedom from the bondage of self. Here you have a new slate to write on.

Six and Seven: Humility

After counting on your fingers to six you realize you are halfway through. Just to be sure you count again. I did it. You the man! Go girl! Yes, numerically, being at six and seven you are halfway through. However, this is neither the end of the beginning nor the beginning of the end. It's a line of demarcation. The battle has only been joined, not won. Starting now, a forever war between the old self and the new self is declared. Mostly these will be skirmishes. However, if not persistent in preventive maintenance, the old self will breach your defenses. To think otherwise is a forlorn hope.

Having passed the Fifth Step final exam, it's only natural to think the hard part is over. Counting on your fingers up to seven, you believe you are halfway through. After a few "I'm sorry" stories and throwing in a couple of bucks, you think this "step thing" is over. All that's left to do is step up to the podium and tell everyone else what they should do. Ah, if only that was so. But it's not. Now is not the time to talk the talk, but to walk the walk. And though the road you are travelling on seems to be going in the right direction there is ahead many a detour, dead end, and one-way streets.

Nor will the old self let go quickly. After a life of fighting tooth and nail not to let go, the old self will never unconditionally surrender. It's battle-hardened and knows guerilla warfare too. When the old self goes to a knife fight, it brings a gun. You'll soon discover you're no saint. Though free of the bondage of self, we still like to roll up in our old blankets. In the future, when the world has you in a stranglehold, find your hands. Most likely they're around your throat. Ahead is a vast no-man's land. It takes discipline to let go. On completion of Step Five, we don't get a halo. We get a chance to start over. And even if by some chance you think you did get a halo, it's only a noose a few inches above your head just waiting to ring your neck.

In referencing the Big Book for the directions on six and seven, you'll note they are short. Each gets only one paragraph. This may suggest there's not much there, but you'd be wrong. Brevity, clarity and simplicity is the best way to communicate to a drunk. Frothy emotional appeals seldom suffice. The message that's going to grab and hold the alcoholic must have depth and weight. At one paragraph apiece, six, seven, and eight do just that.

1. What questions are part of the Fifth Step final exam?
   A. Is our work solid so far?
   B. Are the stones properly in place?
   C. Have we skipped on the cement?
   D. Have we tried to make mortar without sand?
   E. Have we omitted anything?
   F. None of the above
   G. All the above

2. What do we receive in completing the fifth step?

3. At six and seven you are halfway through. But, this is neither the end of the _____ nor the beginning of the end. It's a line of _____.

4. Without persistent preventive maintenance, the old self will breach your _____.

5. True or False? Having passed the Fifth Step final exam, the hard part is over.

6. In travelling the road to happy destiny there lies ahead many a _____, _____, and _____ _____.

7. True or False? Having passed the Fifth Step final exam, the old self let go quickly.

8. Having passed the Fifth Step final exam, you discover you're no _____.

9. On completion of Step Five, we don't get a. _____. We get a chance to _____ _____.

10. In the Big Book steps six and seven each gets only one _____.

Step Six is three questions and a prayer. Working Step Six begins with, "If we can answer to our satisfaction." Answer what? That's a reference to the Fifth Step final exam. The second question is, "Are you ready?" And the third is, "Can He?" If you have admitted, decided, written down a lot, and had a long talk, you can answer in the affirmative. If unsure, or still cling to something, we ask (pray) for help.

Step Seven is a reaffirmation and validation of the deal you made with God in three. It begins, "My Creator." Your Higher Power now has a name. It's no longer a leaf on a tree or a group of drunks. Now that we know who to pray to, we pray for the removal of our defects. Especially those that prevent us from carrying this message and practicing these principles. This step is now complete.

To understand Steps Six and Seven, let's try a sports analogy. In football, each end zone has the name of a team. In this scenario, one is hubris, the other humiliation. The hubris team represents excessive pride, and the humiliation one extreme shame. At the fifty-yard line is you. On the whistle you go. But which way? Once again, you're between a rock and a hard place.

On the field, if an alcoholic quarterback calls the plays, there are no touchdowns. Only turnovers, fumbles, and interceptions. You'll get tackled, pummeled, and flattened. Floundering between the extreme and the excessive, penalty flags fly on every play.

To experience humility, you can't call the plays. The moment you think you are humble, you've fumbled. And for that, there will be a penalty. Hubris is thinking you can take a drink, and humiliation is the result of that drink. Humility is a low-scoring game.

Humility comes from knowing what to do. Being a doormat for others to wipe their feet on is not being humble. That's why the first lesson in humility is understanding that if troubled, go to God at once. If the trouble remains, God wants to teach you something. Humility comes from doing what you don't want to do. And once experienced in doing the right thing for the right reason you'll know what humility is. It's being able to stand tall before the God of your own understanding and knowing you are who you were meant to be. After all, aren't we in the world to play the role He assigns? Being humble is knowing you are worth God's time and love because you earned it.

Uneducated and poor, Lawrence joined Napoleon's Army for food and shoes. In a brightly colored uniform, he, and those like him, lined up in open fields. Once in place, with a flourish of flags, the beat of the drum, and a call of the bugle, they step forward to be scythed down. But, for the grace of God Lawrence survived his enlistment. On his discharge he was once again in need of food and shoes. So, this time thinking it more conducive to a long life he joined a monastery. However, lacking education and holy orders, Brother Lawrence could only serve as a cook and cobbler. From this experience came the book, *The Practice of the Patience of God.* In which he says the marvel of God's grace is abundant and all around us. That even in the most menial of tasks, one will find God's grace imprinted on it. Brother Lawrence advises we don't have to look for it, only to take comfort in it. And in that comfort know the meaning of humility. It's not that hard.

1. The three questions asked in Step Six are?

2. If we still cling to something in step six, what do we do?

3. Step Seven is a _____ and _____ of the deal you made with God in three.

4. What is your Higher Power name in the seventh step prayer?

5. Hubris represents excessive _____ and humiliation extreme _____.

6. On the field, if an alcoholic quarterback calls the plays, there are no _____.

7. The moment you think you are humble, you've _____. And that means a _____.

8. Hubris is thinking you can take a _____, and humiliation is the result of that _____.

9. True or False? Humility being a doormat for others to wipe their feet on.

10. True or False? Humility is being able to stand tall before the God of your own understanding and knowing you are who you were meant to be.

11. On the firing line of life, when an alcoholic steps forward they get _____ _____.

12. In his book, *The Practice of the Patience of God* Brother Lawrence says we should do what?

13. Even in the most menial of tasks, what is imprinted on it.

However, the practice of the presence of God is not easy. Avoid then an over reliance on the intellect and concentrate on developing the strength and the sanity to make it through just one more day. Keep your prayers brief, clear, and simple. Ask not for relief from sorrow but endurance to persevere. With practice the mind can become restrained from the turbulence of wandering worry and woe. Understand that you cannot control what thoughts pop up. Your mind is like a slot machine. All day long it spins and what usually comes up is 'loser'. None the less, you do have control over what to do with those thoughts. You can hold on to them and believe the lies you tell yourself. You can live with them and drift into worry, remorse, and morbid reflection. Or you can go to God at once, talk to someone immediately, make necessary amends quickly, and rapidly turn your thoughts to what is good in your life. With practice, prayer, and a "thy will be done" soon this becomes the switch that turns negative thought off. Yes, someone or something is always waiting to turn that switch on, but from this point on you know what to do.

Being in the present moment means a minute from now never comes, and three seconds ago is ancient history. A set time for prayer has no preference over the spontaneous. God doesn't keep office hours. For when it comes to developing a conscience contact with God, maximizing the minimum effort is more than enough. When a wandering and wondering mind causes a loss of tranquility remember this is part of living life on life terms. Think of it as a text from God to give Him a call. He loves to hear your voice from time to time. That's why we say, "We say to ourselves many times each day "thy will be done." Then we will be in much less danger of excitement, anger, worry, fear, frustration, resentment, envy, jealousy and foolish decisions. And what do we mean by many? Well, that would be a shitload.

Make the ordinary the extraordinary. Abide in the thought that in an emergency you need not break glass. Let no business distract or divert you from enjoying your spiritual experience. Keep in mind that the essence of a spiritual awakening is the simple belief that God could do for you what you cannot do for yourself. To overcome shame, guilt and remorse make going to God directly proportional to how much you want to torture yourself. To counter any sorrow in life, keep in mind the process to follow is spirituality, sobriety, sanity and serenity (SX4).

A novice labors. A master directs. Elimination of the drinking is but a beginning. When we speak of the tools of the program, we refer to a set of specific skills. Skills that are not issued but acquired. We grow in our willingness to do the next right thing not through intellect (our best thinking got us here) but experience. In every task begin with the thought "Thy will be done." Envision from beginning to end, that, "Thou are with me." Pray then for God to join you in the hurly-burly of life. Then with each task done say thanks for the discipline, sanity, and strength provided. Going to God early and often during the day allows you to weather the rise and falls of the day's trials and tribulations. Discipline is having the faith in the knowledge it's okay to change your mind when circumstances warrant it. There are no stones so set in place that God can't move them.

1. True or False? The practice of the presence of God is easy.

2. True or False? Reliance on the intellect is all you need for the strength and the sanity to make it through just one more day.

3. prayers _____, _____, and _____. Ask not for relief from _____ but endurance to persevere.

4. What can you do with negative thoughts that just pop up?

5. You can hold on to them and believe the lies you tell yourself.

6. You can drift into worry, remorse, and morbid reflection.

7. You can go to God at once, talk to someone immediately, make necessary amends quickly, and rapidly turn your thoughts to what is good in your life.

8. What is the switch we use to turn off unwanted thoughts?

9. When we say "thy will be done" we are in much less danger of?
    A. excitement,
    B. anger,
    C. worry,
    D. fear,
    E. frustration,
    F. resentment,
    G. envy,
    H. jealousy
    I. foolish decisions.
    J. All the above

10. To counter any sorrow in life, keep in mind the process to follow is _____, _____, _____, and _____ (SX4).

11. True or False? Discipline is having the faith in the knowledge it's okay to change your mind when circumstances warrant it.

12. There are no _____ so set in place that _____ can't move them.

There is a place where dreamers dream, but never reach for the stars. A place where one comes face to face and eye to eye with the truth about oneself. It's a funny thing about the eyes. You cannot see them without reflection. To see your eyes, they must be mirrored back to you. To see clearly what's inside of you there needs to be effort, concentration, and focus. There can be no quick sideways glance. And when an alcoholic is in their cups, looking into their eyes is a sad sight indeed. For they are going it alone, and therefore must carry the weight of their world on their backs. With each step they get weaker, their burden heavier, and as problems mount up, they become astonishingly difficult to solve. We must have a drink. This is the way it is with us. That is why we understand. And because we understand, we can help you, do as we do, if you want to.

A refusal to ask for help comes from the fear of being found out. It's not that we don't know how, or can't ask for help, but we won't. It's how we are. We would rather die than look bad. Asking for help just looks bad. And when we think we look bad we inflame negative thoughts about ourselves. And when that happens the only solution to every thought that comes up is, "you suck". But that just isn't so. It's not, because to get this far, you have demonstrated you have what it takes to make it. That's why we say, "Don't give up before the miracle happens."

Living in the misery of the day is contrary to being in the present moment. For us there is no middle of the road solution. When God says, "Come to me", you better go. For if you don't, you'll have to wait until the next time such fortune passes your way. And until then, there will be more of the same. A mind run amuck is one perplexed by the consciousness of anxiety and apprehension.

There is no obligation to endure whatever. Confession of shortcomings results in absolution. That is what the steps are all about. They allow us to see, and then remove what is preventing us from breathing in the air of the sunlight of the spirit. Once immersed in the warmth of God's grace, everything that was amiss seems to fall into place. When clothed in His grace everything hard becomes easy. That's why in developing the habit of conversing with God, we must keep it brief, clear and simple. After all God is busy keeping the rings around Saturn and making sure Pluto doesn't slam into Neptune.

Diligence, devotion and discipline will be your new watchwords. Self- inflicted pain on the body and mind is turning your back on God. That's why we say without resignation or reservation, "God Grant me the serenity to accept the things I cannot change. The courage to change the things I can. And the wisdom to know the difference." In other words, give me the strength and the sanity to make it through one more day carrying the burden of my thoughts.

In the fellowship of recovery, we don't shoot our wounded. We also set our prisoners free. From knowing who we are, we know what to do. When you are ready, and the time is right, Providence will step in. Our program of action is a design for living that is not about God, but one that demonstrates the power of God.

1. To see your eyes, they must be _____ back to you.

2. When an alcoholic is in their cups, looking into their eyes is a _____ _____ _____.

3. When carrying the weight of their world on our backs. With each step we get _____, the burden _____, and problems become.

4. And when this happens what must we have?

5. A refusal to ask for help comes from the fear of _____ _____ _____.

6. When we think we look bad we inflame _____ _____ about ourselves.

7. Living in the misery of the day is contrary to being in the _____ _____.

8. True or False? For us there is no middle of the road solution.

9. In conversing with God, keep it _____, _____ and _____.

10. In completing step seven _____, _____, and _____ are the new watchwords

11. Saying the Serenity Prayer gives us the _____ and the _____ to make it through one more day.

12. Our program of action is a design for living that is not about God, but one that demonstrates the _____ _____ _____

The foundation of a spiritual life is in holding yourself in the same esteem as God does. Reject the thoughts that you are not enough. Acknowledge the wretchedness of denying and inflaming negative thoughts about yourself. Humility comes from believing that with 8 billion people on the planet it's unlikely you suck more than everyone else. Remember God is invested in you. You are worth his time and effort.

Discharge your daily duties, not to the best of your ability, but with all your ability. Humility is demonstrated by getting up after being knocked down. There is no stronger inducement needed than the argument of purpose. Be calm in the exclusion of the noise and clatter of persistent unwanted thought. We all fail in this endeavor. However, being convinced that the spiritual solution is now at hand, we can impress upon ourselves God's will for us. And what is God's will for us? That He be allowed into our hearts and mind so He may better do His work. Elaborate than on the meditations that come to you when in mental turmoil. God is not out to hurt you but to help you. Believing you are deserving of contempt when trouble thoughts arise, subjects you to the numbness of contradiction and confusion. Make no mistake about this, God is on your side.

We cannot be indifferent to the way we achieve our ends. Not all is possible, but much is probable. Therefore, do not sacrifice what is achievable in pursuit of the impossible. If you try to move a mountain all at once you will get nowhere. But if you labor daily moving that mountain one shovelful at a time, eventually you will see progress. Just imagine how far you can go given that you have got this far already?

Prayer, be it appointed or spontaneous, makes no difference. Sanctification comes not from what we think, but what we think about our thinking. When there is discourse in the brain there is pain of the heart. Accustomed to discouragement and renumeration of this reaction the last thing on our mind is to go to God. Could it be we are too ashamed of our thoughts, words, deeds, and actions to connect with God. If so, fear not. God already knows what you have done.

Do you screen calls? God doesn't. God will never block your number, hang up on you, or put you on hold. His voicemail is never full, He reads your tweets, and responds to emails. And while he doesn't know what a Kardashian is, He can tweet, text, skype, Instagram, and tik-tok all at once. But God doesn't do Facebook. Why? Because a wise man (me) once said, "No good will ever come from Facebook." Don't you just love it when everyone knows you're right?

Still, God knows your number and where you live. There is no escape. Nowhere to run, no place to hide. He'll keep calling you. You best answer. And when told to come along, go quietly.

But how would you feel if you asked God for help and heard, "I'm busy, call back later?" If you think God is out to get you, you're right. But not in the way you think. He's out to get you back. At this phase of your development, you don't need to hear about God; you need to hear, from God. So, when God calls pick up the phone. For it is in conversation with God, you recognize that when in doubt you are being primed to receive His grace.

1. The foundation of a spiritual life is in holding yourself in the same _____ as God does.

2. Humility comes from knowing that with 8 billion people on the planer _____ _____ you suck more than everyone else.

3. Discharge your daily duties, not to the best of your ability, but with _____ _____ _____.

4. Humility is demonstrated by getting up after being _____ _____.

5. Believing you are deserving of _____ when trouble thoughts arise, subjects you to the numbness of contradiction and confusion.

6. Do not sacrifice what is _____ in pursuit of the _____.

7. True or False? Prayer, be it appointed or spontaneous, makes no difference. Sanctification comes not from what we _____, but what we think about our _____.

8. True or False? God will never block your number, hang up on you, or put you on hold.

9. At this phase of your _____ you don't need to hear about God; you need to hear from God.

10. So then, without discouragement when troubled, offer God thanks for all that's good. In this way you are guaranteed to receive more of the same.

Holiness needs no ceremony, no formal training, and no spiritual anointment. Pope or pauper, God shares His Grace with us. Faith in God requires no superior skills. It's in ordinary faith, where extraordinary devotion is found. Faith is the benefit of experience. Those who hold themselves back from the sunlight of the Spirit will never feel the warmth of the sun. And those who fly too high suffer Icarus' fate. It doesn't have to be one or the other.

We acknowledge this experience by noting the wording of the steps. Look at Six. It begins with the word "Were". Which is the past tense of the verb "to be." So now this step is, "To be entirely ready." Like a paratrooper you're prepared to go on order, and that's a humbling phenomenon for sure. Yet, this unassuming experience draws no attention.

She was no longer "Comrade." Convicted of Soviet Article-58, a socially dangerous element, she was now a "Zek." In Stalin's Siberian gulag work camps, one in eight prisoners were women. Her most protected possession was her spoon. Without it, she could not eat. And if she could not eat, she would die. What was her crime? Being the wife, mistress, mother, daughter, or friend of men deemed enemies of the State. Every day she worked. Every night she cried. Whatever the crime, in times like these, only God could dry her tears and loan her a smile.

Recovery is a process of deflation. It won't happen without setbacks. The genesis of humility is defeat. Expect to fall short. Remember, "We are not saints," and that's why we have Step Ten and Eleven. You cannot create self-esteem out of nothing. It's built up from doing trivial things. The ones you're supposed to do. To become a woman of grace and dignity, show up after the humiliation.

God is not concerned with perfection; God doesn't make junk. It's you who trashed your life. In the inventory phase, you bagged up all that garbage and tossed it into the dumpster. Then, as soon as something doesn't go your way, you go dumpster diving for a well-worn defect. You define the moment by your response. You can't train to be humble. Humility comes from doing what you don't want to do without complaint or want of praise. That's why a "thy will be done" at the right time can save the day. Act immediately and the present becomes the past. If you choose to walk around with crap on your shoe, you'll take it wherever you go.

Old behaviors return not because you did something wrong, they return to remind you God is there for you. God only removes those defects of character that stand in the way of your usefulness to others. Leaving you with some flaws assures you will return for His help as you help others. It's from your failures your spirituality grows. God can do for you what you can't do for yourself.

1. In thanking God for all that's good what are guaranteed?

2. Holiness needs no _____, no formal _____, and no spiritual _____.

3. True or False? Pope or pauper, God shares His Grace with us. True

4. It's in _____ faith, where _____ devotion is found.

5. Recovery is a process of _____.

6. The genesis of humility is _____.

7. Because we are not saints we to have _____ _____ and _____.

8. True or False? You create self-esteem by doing the trivial things.

9. How do you become a woman of grace and dignity?

10. A _____ _____ _____ _____ at the right time can save the day.

11. Why do old behaviors return?

Thus, the first rule with humility is to regret it, then forget it. Deadwood only yields fresh growth after flame ravages a forest. It's in the charred remains we find God's work. He never leaves us wanting and always returns what is lost. Where God is concerned, finding humility is like receiving a spiritual hug. It's one you deserve. All you must do is leave for God what is God's business and take care of what's yours.

Bringing selfishness into contact with humility causes enormous emotional and mental displacement. For protection, you clothe yourself in psychological armor, arming yourself with weapons for self-destruction. Not wanting to look foolish is a prime human motivator. Many character defects are personal defenses. Humility is not belittling yourself. Cutting yourself down is self-centered pride masquerading as humility. Being a doormat is not humble. If you put yourself down all the time, you're inviting people to wipe their feet on you. Yet, be you humbled or humiliated, you can stop drinking. That is, if you do as you're told.

Here, the guiding principle that once drove our life is cast aside and replaced with a new set of means and motives. God is now our host, and we are no longer a hostage. Now we know we can go to God to flip off the switch that controls the peculiar mental twist.

While these steps remove your defects of character, no step takes away your human nature. Humility is not being free of trials, tribulations, and defects of character. Humility is an awareness that you can stand tall in front of God without fear, realizing you are worth it. As said before, completing these steps doesn't get you a halo. And even if you get one, that halo above your head is only inches away from being a noose around your neck. All you are getting when you sound off: "My Creator, I am now willing that you can have all of me," is a chance to start over.

Letting go of religion does not mean you let go of God. There is no need to look for God in the grandest of churches. He is in the closet, the cupboard, the freezer, and the shoebox under your bed. When you get a gift from God, it's not always wrapped up nicely. Do not discount the influence of external icons. Don't re-gift that Christmas candle; light it and invite God into your day. Seeing that flame flicker as you putter around will remind you that God is watching over you.

In the Seventh Step Prayer, you may wonder why you must give up the good and the bad? To answer this, refer to Step Five, where we're told to tell "*all* our life story." There is a reason "*all*" is italicized. It's this: "All the king's horses and all the king's men couldn't put Humpty Dumpty together again." But God could and would, but only if you give Him all the pieces.

Completing this step, like going to Jump School, changes your life. It's time to put your training into action. If you have been diligent in development, you are ready; God is willing, the time is right, and everything is prepared. This is it! Let's go! It's time to hurry up and wait.

1. The first rule of humility is to _____ _____, then _____ _____.

2. True or False? God never leaves us wanting and always returns what is lost. T

3. True or False? Where God is concerned, finding humility is like receiving a spiritual hug.

4. To practice humility all you must do is leave for God what is God's _____ and take care of what's yours.

5. Bringing _____ into contact _____ with causes enormous emotional and mental displacement.

6. True or False? If you put yourself down all the time, you're inviting people to wipe their feet on you.

7. True or False? Humility is being free of trials, tribulations, and defects of character.

8. When God becomes your host, you are no longer a _____.

9. Letting go of _____ does not mean you let go of God.

10. In the Seventh Step Prayer, why do we ask God to take both the good and the bad?

11. If you have been diligent in development, you are _____ ready; God is _____, and the time is _____.

12 and 12 Step Five

Admitted to God, to ourselves, and another human being the exact nature of our wrongs. Or is it defects?

All 12 steps deflate the ego. And no other step is like step five. For its successful consummation we will need a witness. One that understands what we are doing and why it is necessary. It's to them, we will reveal those tormenting ghosts of yesterday we'd rather not remember.

In our inventory we sweep the searchlight over our lives. While discovering much, little is resolved. You see, even with the completion of the fourth step we still have no peace of mind. We still carry our character defects with us. We have bagged them up, but not properly disposed of them. We must talk to somebody. However, pride and fear exacerbate a desire to skimp on this step. We search for an easier, softer way. One which comprises a general admission, that when drinking, we made some mistakes. A revelation our family, friends and employers already know. But regarding our deepest and darkest secrets, we are reluctant to let them again see the light of day. Wasn't writing them down enough of a penance? As such, there may remain a determination to take these distressing and humiliating memories to the grave with us. Not a soul shall know our secrets.

This is unwise. For without the uncompromising completion of this vital step there remains a threat to long-term sobriety. Nothing will hinder your spiritual growth more than holding back on step five. Many who avoid this step relapse. Even old-timers who have failed to clean house pay dearly. Having skimped on the cement put into the foundation, any structure built on it remains in danger of collapse from the mildest of misdirected winds. These type simply cannot find relief from the very character defects they are trying to conceal. This stolen valor of sobriety without serenity leads to irritability, anxiety, shame, guilt, remorse, and depression.

The practice of confession is ancient and validated. Psychiatrists and psychologists explain to those they treat that gaining insight into one's personality flaws is not only a practical form of treatment but one that offers permanent relief. That by discussing our shortcomings with others, we lighten the burden we carry. But for the alcoholic, we must go even further. We must make a fearless admission of all our defects. Otherwise, the grace of God cannot enter our life and expel our obsession with alcohol.

What do you receive from step five? We get rid of isolation. Even before drinking got bad, we never felt like we belonged. Either we were noisy good fellows craving attention or were sulking depressants hiding in the shadows. Regardless of where one falls on the spectrum, without exception, loneliness tortures alcoholics. A type of loneliness that raises a mysterious barrier that can only be lowered with the intake of alcohol. For without a drink, we have no idea which way to go. It's a problem we can never surmount nor understand. Like an actor who can't remember their line, without the ease and comfort of alcohol, we felt terrified and lonely. But eventually, even Bacchus boomerangs on us.

1. All 12 steps _____ _____ _____.

2. For its successful consummation of step five we need a _____..

3. What is it they witness?

4. Searching for an easier, softer way, _____ and _____ exacerbate a desire to skimp on this step.

5. Regarding our deepest and darkest secrets, we are _____ to let them see the light of day.

6. Why is it after the completion of the fourth step we still have no peace of mind?

7. Nothing will hinder your _____ _____ more than holding back on step five.

8. The stolen valor of sobriety without serenity leads to.
    A. irritability,
    B. anxiety,
    C. shame,
    D. guilt,
    E. remorse,
    F. depression
    G. All of the above

9. True or False? The practice of confession is ancient and validated. True

10. By discussing our shortcomings with others, we lighten the _____ _____ _____.

11. We must make a _____ _____ of all our _____ for the grace of God to enter our life and expel our obsession with alcohol.

12. What do you receive from step five?

13. Without the ease and comfort of alcohol, we felt _____ and _____.

When we got to AA, we found people who understood. There was a sense of belonging. We thought it solved the isolation problem. But while not alone in the social sense, we still suffered the old pangs of anxious avoidance. We had to talk to somebody about this conflict. Even more so, we had to listen to someone else do the same. Step five is the answer. Involvement in this step establishes our kinship with man and God. It puts us on solid footing as being one among many.

Step five begins the forgiveness process. It is while working on this step we sense forgiveness for those who deeply wronged us. Although our moral inventory persuades us forgiveness is desirable. It is only after completing step five, that we too receive forgiveness, for we now recognize our deficiencies is being part of the human condition. For many of us, this is our first experience with humility. This first taste of humility, a word often misunderstood, is the dividend of step five. This is the recognition of who you are. For only by knowing who you are and why you are like that can you understand why it is important to change.

In reading our inventory, we suspect our troubles are of our own making. This comes from the revelation we fooled ourselves into believing we were not deceiving ourselves. What's even more astonishing is the effort we made in trying to deceive God.

Having gone back over our lives being thorough and honest, this is only a peek into our past. We remain beset with delusions of grandeur. And while step five is a humbling experience, it doesn't mean freedom from self-will. Our defects remain. We did not push them away. We only made an admission. Therefore, something more is required.

Thus, the admission of our defects, like the elimination of drinking, is but a beginning. It is not enough to get by the shame, guilt, and remorse we harbor. In making our admission, being very much the actor, we will sometimes dramatize and exaggerate our shortcomings. It's from behind the smokescreen generated by pride and fear liabilities great and small remain hidden. This is the distressing selfishness and self-centeredness we don't even know we have.

Therefore, a solitary self-appraisal is not enough. We need to hear the truth from God and another human being. Only by holding nothing back and accepting direction do we attain genuine humility. Yet many still can't understand why we need to involve other people.

At this stage, many a defect of character remain hidden, and our willingness to clean house is but theoretical. Having come to realize that God knows all that we have done and has forgiven us makes being alone with God less embarrassing. This makes dealing only with God problematic. Going it alone in spiritual matters is dangerous. We must sit down and talk honestly with another person in order to confirm we have been honest with God. Doing this now prepares us for the tough work of setting right our wrongs in the ninth step.

1. When we got to AA, we found people who _____.

2. To avoid the pangs of anxious avoidance we had to talk to somebody about this _____.

3. True or False? Involvement in this step establishes our kinship with man and God. It puts us on solid footing as being one among many.

4. Step five begins the _____ process.

5. In completing step five, we recognize our _____ as being part of the human condition.

6. For many of us, participating in step five is our first _____ _____ _____.

7. True or False? While step five is a humbling experience, it doesn't mean freedom from self-will.

8. The smokescreen generated by pride and fear hides _____ big and small.

9. The most distressing form of selfishness and self-centeredness is the type we don't _____ _____ _____ _____.

10. Going it alone in spiritual matters is _____.

11. We sit down and talk honestly with another person to confirm we"ve been _____ with God.

12. Doing the fifth prepares us for setting _____ _____ _____ _____ in the ninth step.

In a solitary self-appraisal, our intentions and motivations can be garbled. It's from talking to another person, we learn to tell the true from the false. Without such an experience wishful thinking and rationalization can camouflage the facts. Lacking practice and humility many well-intentioned people will claim a connection with God. Mostly, they are sorely mistaken. And instead try to justify the most errant nonsense because they claim they are only doing as God wills. This makes for foolish, perhaps tragic blunders.

Spiritual development comes from discussing matters of importance with others before acting. This is especially good advice to those new to establishing a constant contact with God.

Once we decide to disclose ourselves to another, the question arises in whom this will be. We must take much care here. For prudence is a virtue that not all have. Remember, we are to share what not everyone ought to know. We will want someone with experience, is sober, and who has surmounted their own difficulties. This could be your sponsor, or perhaps not. It may turn out that a priest, doctor, or total stranger may be best. It's only important we choose someone whose temperament is that of an intimate confidant and that they will not reveal your story. While we make no rule, we suggest you takes as soon as possible after completing the writing.

The actual test will be in your willingness to completely confide in the one you choose. No one says the AA program requires no willpower, it requires all you've got. It takes great resolution to place your trust in someone else. However, if carefully explained, the recipient of your confidence will soon become eager. They may even tell a story about themselves. This should place you at ease at holding nothing back.

When finished there is a sense of indescribable relief. Many years of dammed-up negative emotions about yourself and others will completely vanish. As the pain subsides, a healing tranquility takes its place. There is a sense that humility and serenity are at hand. This is the reward of doing this work.

Often with the agnostic and atheist step five provides more than relief of bondage of self. There is a feeling that one is emerging from isolation. From the open and honest sharing of guilt and remorse there comes a sense of forgiveness. But forgiveness from whom or what? Could it be sharing brings us to a resting place where the possibility of God exists? Is this the clarity of thought we call sobriety?

1. In a solitary self-appraisal, our _____ and _____ can be garbled.

2. Wishful thinking and rationalization can _____ the facts.

3. Lacking practice and humility many well-intentioned people will try to justify the most errant nonsense claiming _____ _____ _____ _____ _____.

4. Spiritual development comes from _____ _____ _____ _____ before taking action.

5. In deciding whom to disclose ourselves to, the question arises in _____ _____ _____ _____.

6. Prudence is _____ a that not all have.

7. It's important we choose someone whose temperament is that of an _____ _____ who will not reveal your story.

8. When finished with the fifth step there is a sense of _____ _____.

9. What is the reward of doing this work?

10. From the open and honest sharing of guilt and remorse there comes _____.

12 and 12 Step 6

Getting to Step Six proves you've come a long way spiritually. As it says, up until this point we may have had certain spiritual beliefs, but now we *begin* to have a spiritual experience. The question of God is, or he isn't, is solved. Having achieved some degree of clarity of thought about the causes and conditions of what we are like, why we are like that, and why it's important to change we are ready to take step six without reservation. We are ready to remove the chains that hold us in the bondage of self.

This proposition is not theory. For we are now sure God could do for us, what we cannot do for ourselves. Having been beaten into a sense of reasonableness we are now ready to try something else. From the work done this far we realize our willpower is of no avail. A change of scenery and the best efforts of family, friends, doctors, and clergy got us no place. We simply could not stop drinking because no human power can cure alcoholism. We had to clean house. We had to ask God for help. We had to accept the three pertinent ideas of, I can't, you can't, but God could. Only then does the obsession vanish.

In meetings, statements such as these we hear every day. In their own way each member of Alcoholics Anonymous is a miracle of healing. They come to the fellowship looking for a solution, a way out. In this literal way, each AA is entirely ready to have God remove every defect of character the very day they walk through the door. And this is exactly what God will do.

Having relief from alcoholism, why then should we not be able to achieve the same with every other defect? The answer to this riddle is apparent to us. For only God can do for us that we cannot do for ourselves.

When a person with alcoholism pours alcohol into themselves, they commit suicide on the installment plan. In the process of destroying their lives they lose any desire for self-preservation. During the many phases of self-destruction, they grasp desperately for any lifeline. Having grabbed hold of our manner of living and sensing they are saved; they believe the next time will be different. So, they let go. They fail to understand that once an alcoholic, always an alcoholic. We are like men who have lost their legs.

Let us be clear about our solution; something more than human power is needed if we are to re-create our life. Only by the grace of God are we not only able to expel the obsession with alcohol but to live a happy, healthy and whole existence. This promise alone provides reasons for existence. This is a new way of life for us. We used to think one way and now we think another.

After the fifth step most of our difficulties remain. Why is this? Because our alcoholism is with us drunk or sober. Every person wants to be somebody and wishes for safety and security. God did not design man to destroy himself. Our Creator expects us to live as human beings with warts and all. This is human nature. It's when these desires exceed the intended purposes, we seek more satisfaction and pleasure then due us. Here we depart from God's wish for us and take on the demands of self.

1. Getting to Step Six proves you've come a long way _____.

2. Up until Step Six we may have had certain spiritual beliefs, but now we _____ to have a spiritual experience.

3. Arriving at this point we achieve a degree of clarity of thought of.

   - What we are_____

   - Why we are _____ _____

   - Why it's _____ ____ _____

4. In six we are ready to remove the chains that hold us in _____ ____ _____.

5. We simply can't stop drinking because no human power can _____ _____.

6. To achieve sobriety, we had to _____ _____ and accept ____ _____ _____.

7. In their own way each member of Alcoholics Anonymous is a _____ ____ _____.

8. When a person with alcoholism pours alcohol into themselves, they _____ _____ on the _____ _____.

9. Having grabbed hold of our manner of living and sensing they are saved; why do people let go?

10. Like men who have lost their legs; once an _____, always an _____.

11. Only by the _____ _____ _____ are we not only able to expel the obsession with alcohol.

12. What is the basis of our new way of life?

If we ask God to forgive our dereliction, it will be done. However, we will never be as white as snow. Being entirely ready means working towards obtainable objectives. God only asks that we do the best we can, and make progress in the building of character.

So, step six, being entirely ready is AA's way of beginning a lifetime job. This does not mean that it will lift all our character defects out of us as the desire to drink is. The keyword of being ready is what we aim for. At first, few have this degree of readiness. The best we can do is try to have the strength and the sanity to make it through one more day. It is only human to say, "No, I can't give this up yet." Why this reluctance? How is it possible to defy the will of God? Where do we get this power if lack of power is our dilemma?

Yes, God is most powerful. The creator and overseer of the universe. But there is one power that can circumvent the will of God. That power is self-will. And the reason self-will is so powerful is that God gave it to us. For you see by having the power of self, God is assured He will hear from you. So, no matter how far we progress, there will always be a natural desire to oppose the will of God and shun His grace. This is what separates mankind from the rest of His creations.

Everybody wishes to be rid of destructive handicaps. No one wants to be a braggart, greedy, angry, or gluttonous. No one wants the agony of chronic pain. No one wants to continually fail or be paralyzed by sloth. While most of us do not hit rock bottom, we need not congratulate ourselves. After all, the reason we arrive at the door is for self-preservation and to avoid punishment, not spiritual involvement.

But once through the door we realize that in order to stay sober we must face up to the fact that we exalt in our defects. We love them. Who doesn't feel superior to the next person? Isn't it true we say, when we get as bad as that fellow we'll quit? Do we not let greed masquerade as ambition? Is it not true we speak love with our lips with lust in our minds? We see self-righteous anger as enjoyable. We take satisfaction out of annoying other people. For it brings us a feeling of superiority. The same is true of gossip. This form of character assassination has the satisfaction of not only criticizing but proclaiming our own self-righteousness.

We live in a world riddled with doubt. It infects everybody, and consumes substantial amounts of time wishing for salvation, rather than working for it. When it comes to quitting drinking, the leveling of our pride, confession of shortcomings, and implementing a spiritual solution, we alcoholics are masters of procrastination.

In the fifth step we submit a lengthy list of defects. We say we are now ready for God to take them all away. However, after the initial delight wears off few seriously think of giving them all up. We want to pick and choose what we give up. This is because many of us conclude just not drinking is more than enough. They have met the demands of others. Didn't they just tell us to stop drinking? Having done so, why then should we give up the psychological armor that has protected us for so long? We prefer to stay in the security blankets that protect us from the truth about ourselves. We settle for getting a check mark in the stop drinking block.

1. Being entirely ready means working towards _____ ..

2. True or False? Step six is the beginning a lifetime job.

3. When it comes to this step it is only human to say,

4. How is it possible to defy the will of God?

5. Why did God give us self-will?

6. Being human there is a natural desire to _____ the will of God and _____ His grace.

7. The reason we arrive at the door of AA is for _____ and to avoid _____.

8. To stay sober, we must face up to the fact that we _____ _____ _____ _____.

9. Gossip is a form of character assassination has the satisfaction of not only _____ but proclaiming our own _____.

10. When it comes to _____ we alcoholics are masters of procrastination.

- the leveling of ____ _____
- confession of _____ and
- implementing a _____ _____

If pressed to do more, we are quick to point out its progress not perfection. That the difference between the men and the boys is one seeks self-centered objectives and the other aims for perfection. Step six is not the achievement of perfection. It's but a beginning. Not of perfection but of humility. For perfection is only possible for God. And perfect humility is not possible for man. Thus, we seize on this reasoning to justify holding on to some of our worst items in stock.

Only in step one does humility merge with perfection. After that our human condition takes over. That's why we need steps ten and eleven. They are the measuring sticks of our progress. Seen in this light, step six is still difficult, but not impossible. It is only urgent that we understand that what we are doing is fulfilling the agreement we made with God in the third step. We again need to be reminded that half-measures get us nothing. There is more to sobriety than just not drinking. It's a different way of life, it's a different way of thinking.

The advantage of completing step six is a venture into open-mindedness. Yes, we need to raise our eyes towards perfection and to walk in that direction. However, the only questions to be answered at this moment are: Have we answered to our satisfaction? Are we now ready? Can He take our defects away? Having invited God into the process we can answer "yes" to all.

Looking at our defects, we now ask if we are unconstitutionally willing to give them up? Maybe we can postpone or indefinitely delay giving them *all* up? After all there is no hard and fast rule that we must give them up. We are only obliged to want to give them up. This contradiction to accept imperfection seems open-ended. This won't do. For with apprehension and doubt about the directions we are only blocking ourselves with rationalization. A rationalization that has proven faulty. We must come to grips with our worst defects of character and act toward their removal as quickly as possible. The moment we say no, never, or wait, our mind snaps close to the grace of God. This is dangerous. If we value our newfound faith, we are ready to abandon our self-centered ways and move toward God's will for us. This we do in the seventh step.

1. When pressed, we are quick to point out its _____ _____ _____.

2. What differentiates the men from the boys?

3. True or False? Step six is the attainment of perfection.

4. True or False? Perfection is only possible for God.

5. Since perfect humility isn't possible, we use this reasoning to justify holding on to what?

6. In what step one does humility merge with perfection?

7. Steps ten and eleven are used for measuring our _____.

8. There is more to sobriety than just not drinking. It's a different way of _____; it's a different way of _____. life; thinking

9. Completing step six is a venture into _____.

10. Looking at our defects, we are now _____ _____ to give them up?

11. True or False? There is no rule that we must give up our shortcomings, only to be ready to do so.

12. What questions do we ask in step six?

    - Have we answered to our _____?

    - Are we now _____?

    - Can He take our _____ _____?

12 and 12 Step Seven

We cannot live useful lives of purpose in adversity if we only summon God into our lives when in distress. Step Seven concerns itself with humility. What is the meaning of this word, and how do we practice it? Indeed, the attainment of humility is the foundation of each of AA's 12 steps. For without humility, no alcoholic can stay sober. Yet, in our past life, we have found this precious quality doesn't leave much room for being happy, joyous, and free as defined by the selfishness and self-centeredness we don't even know we have. For we cannot imagine life either with or without alcohol.

Humility is an ideal. One that's often seen as a handicap in this world. Do not misunderstand. Many people have no idea that humility is a way of life. After all, history highlights man's pride in his achievements. With great intelligence, men of science and education harness, process, and devour resources in such quantity that man-made peace and happiness is at hand. That poverty will disappear, and war will be something of the past. That security and satisfaction will be abundant. Our primary instincts will be satisfied and there won't be anything to quarrel about. We will be free to concentrate on culture and character. By our intelligence and labor, we will shape our destiny.

Certainly, no member of AA wants to deprecate material achievement. Nor do we debate whether the belief or the necessity to satisfy natural desires is the chief objective of life. But we are sure that no class of people has ever made a bigger mess of things trying to live by this formula. We drink to dream grand dreams. Then, when frustrated, even in part, we drink for oblivion. There is never enough of what we want. Even when well-intentioned our crippling handicap is a lack of humility. We lack the perspective to see that character-building and spiritual values must come first. We go all-out consuming instead of regarding satisfaction with what we have been given to be the aim of life.

Though most of us desire humility, we cannot conjure up the honesty required. What we are really after is what we want. And given the choice between character and comfort, we leave the character in the dust. We only think of making honesty, tolerance, and love of man our goal when it will benefit us.

This lack of anchorage to values blinds us to the true purpose of our lives. In pursuit of personal happiness, we often produce poor results. We try to live only by our strength and intelligence. The need for a higher power just isn't there. Even when we believe God exists, we still play God ourselves. And if we place self-reliance above God-reliance, happiness is out of the question. The basic ingredient of humility, which is a desire to do God's will, is missing. How than can we induce this need into ourselves?

For us, gaining a new perspective is painful. It's from successive humiliating defeats we are forced to consider what humility is all about. Only then do we feel that humility is something more than groveling despair. Ask any newcomer and they will tell you a humble admission of being powerless over alcohol is only the first step away from its paralyzing grip.

1. Step Seven concerns itself with _____.

2. Without humility, no alcoholic can stay _____.

3. Why can't an alcoholic stay sober without humility?

4. True or False? Humility as an ideal is often seen as a handicap in this world.

5. True or False? Humility is defined as with great intelligence, men of science and education harness, process, and devour resources in such quantity that man-made peace and happiness is at hand.

6. Alcoholics, as a class of people, always seem to make a _____ _____ _____.

7. When frustrated, even in part, we drink for _____ because there is never enough of _____ _____ _____.

8. Though most of us desire, _____ we cannot conjure up the _____ required.

9. What blinds us to the true purpose of our lives?

10. When we place self-reliance above God-reliance what is out of the question?

11. What is the basic ingredient of humility?

12. It's only from _____ _____ _____ are we forced to consider what humility is all about.

13. A humble admission of being powerless over alcohol is only the _____ _____ away from its paralyzing grip.

So, we see humility as a necessity. But this concept is unknown. For even in sobriety, our vision of being humble comes from a lifetime of selfishness and self-centeredness. This we cannot set in reverse all at once. For rebellion dogs every step we take on the road to happy destiny. Though we believe, humbly and without reservation, we are powerless over alcohol, this is but the first step in passing over the Bridge to Reason. We think just not drinking is enough. Thank God that is over and done with. Then we learn to our consternation that this is only the first step on the road we are walking. Courted by the sheer necessity, we reluctantly come to grips with our character flaws that made us problem drinkers.

We must deal with these flaws to prevent relapse. We want to be rid of these defects but recoil from the idea of doing the work. It will cost us too much if we keep disturbing our equilibrium. How can we possibly summon the resolution to be rid of our human compulsions and desires?

But by now we are driven by the inescapable conclusion we draw from our alcoholic experience. We must try with all our will, or else, fall by the wayside. This puts us under heavy pressure to do the right thing. Under the penalties of failure, we take this step grudgingly. We may still see humility as an undesirable personal trait, but we recognize its necessity for our survival. So, we take it.

When looking at our defects and discussing them with another, we begin to gain some clarity of thought. For by this time, we have gained a measure of release. We enjoy peace of mind. The depression and anxiety that once constructed our very existence is gone. Where hubris and humiliation once force fed us humble pie, now in its place is the gift of spirituality, sobriety, sanity, and serenity. This is our experience. It can be yours too.

This new perception is a revolutionary change in our outlook. Our eyes open and we come to grips with the painful ego puncturing. Until now, we have devoted our lives to running from pain. In the past, we dealt with suffering via the bar and the bottle. Character building, as opposed to avoiding suffering, doesn't appeal to us. Then we learned to listen and to listen to learn. We see humility transforms misery into peace and prosperity. We hear story after story about how humility brought strength out of weakness. That the antidote to pain is to feel the pain. That it only takes a small measure of faith to desire humility.

In learning about humility, there is a change in our attitude toward God. This is true if we had been believers or not. We get over the idea that God is only to be called upon in an emergency. The notion we could live by only having God's help from time to time evaporates. We are no longer confused by what humility is or it isn't. We understand the meaning of the words "of myself, I am nothing."

We can't be bludgeoned into humility. It must come voluntarily. This is a significant turning point in our lives. For in seeking humility as something we want, rather than need, we can now commence with living life on life's terms. This marks the time when we unreservedly beseech God to remove our shortcomings.

1. For the alcoholic humility is a _____.

2. But even in sobriety our vision of being humble comes from a lifetime of _____ and _____.

3. True or False? Rebellion dogs every step we take on the road to happy destiny.

4. True or False? It is our character flaws that made us problem drinkers.

5. Why do we recoil from the idea of doing the work?

6. When discussing our defects with others we begin to gain _____ _____ _____.

7. Where hubris and humiliation once force fed us humble pie, now in its place is.
   - spirituality,
   - sobriety,
   - sanity,
   - serenity
   - All the above
   - None of the above

8. Coming to grips with the painful ego puncturing there is a _____ _____ in our outlook.

9. True or False? Character building, as opposed to avoiding suffering, doesn't appeal to us.

10. We _____ to listen and to listen to _____.

11. That the _____ to pain, is to feel the pain.

12. True or False? We can be bludgeoned into humility.

13. Step Seven marks the time when we beseech God to remove our _____.

In taking step seven, what is our objective? It's assurance the grace of God can do for us, what we cannot do for ourselves. We have seen the shortsightedness and the obstacles that block our path. We no longer make unreasonable demands upon ourselves. The chief activator of our defects has been selfishness, self-centeredness, and primarily fear. Having lived in a state of continual disturbance and frustration due to unsatisfied demands, we are now at peace. We have come to realize there is a difference between a demand and a request.

In the seventh step, we ask that God remove our defects of character. The whole emphasis of Step Seven is so that we may better do His will. And in so doing there is the removal of our shortcomings, meaning we are no longer powerless over alcohol or the thoughts, words, deeds, and actions of others. Instead, a power greater than ourselves has restored us to sanity with humility. We have discovered that where there is hope, there is God. And where there is God there is peace of mind.

Steps Five, Six and Seven Closeout

Having made an inventory what do we do with it? For like with Step Three, without a vigorous follow through there is little permanent effect. While the work up to this point is difficult, it is not punishment. It's needed to develop a new attitude and relationship with our Creator. Hence forth we used to think one way, and now we think another.

Completing the fifth we learn what the source of our trouble is. It is of our own making. It was not the drinking, but our thinking. Self-reliance convinced us the solution to problems lies at the bottom of a bottle. We just didn't know any better. Now having ascertained what the obstacles are, we can see that the road to God's house is open to all. There, the door is always open, and nobody gets thrown out. All we need do is knock.

It is by knocking on the door of six, and entering through seven, we see the solution in brief, clear, and simple terms. Just not drinking works great for not getting drunk. But when it comes to living life on life terms just not drinking has a shelf live. Over time it sours. Having persevered with the don't drink, go to meetings and ask for help part of the program, many still fail. They understand the program of action is simple but refuse to throw their life-long conceptions out the window.

It's in six and seven we turn our will, which is the way we think, and our lives, the way we act, over to the care and protection of a God. And in so doing, not only is our drinking problem removed, but all our defects are gone too. We have a clean slate to write on. We have followed through on the deal we made with God in Step Three.

This we know because we have followed the clear-cut simple directions contained in the book from which the fellowship takes its name. Directions, that if followed, will not only expel the obsession for alcohol, but allow the practitioner to live a happy, healthy, and whole existence. But now we need more action, for faith without work is death.

1. What is our objective in Step Seven?

2. The chief activator of our defects is.
   - selfishness
   - self-centeredness
   - fear
   - All the above

3. True or False? There is no difference between a demand and a request.

4. In the seventh step, we ask that God remove our _____ ____ _____.

5. The emphasis of Step Seven is so that we may _____ ____ _____ _____.

6. And in so doing we are no longer powerless over alcohol or the _____, _____, _____, and _____ of others.

7. In Step Seven God restored us to _____ ____ _____.

8. Where there is hope, there is _____. And where there is God is _____.

9. Completing the fifth we learn what the _____ _____ _____ _____ _____.

10. In six and seven we turn our will, which is the _____ _____ _____ and our lives, which is the _____ _____ _____ over to the care and protection of a God.

11. Completing the fourth through the seventh steps reaffirms we have followed through with what?

Big Book Step Study Format

Step 1, Part 1	Admitted we were powerless	*The Doctor's Opinion*
Step 1, Part 2	Our lives were unmanageable	*More About Alcoholism*
Step 2, Part 1	Came to believe	*We Agnostics*
Step 2, Part 2	Restored to sanity	*There Is a Solution*
Step 3	Made a decision	*How It Works* (p.58-64)
Step 4, Part 1	Resentment Inventory	*How It Works* (p.64-67)
Step 4, Part 2	Fear Inventory	*How It Works* (p.67-68)
Step 4, Part 3	Sex Inventory	*How It Works* (p.68-71)
Step 5	Admitted to God and another	*Into Action* (p.72-75)
Step 6	Were entirely ready	*Into Action* (p.76, paragraph 1)
Step 7	Humbly asked	*Into Action* (p.76, paragraph 2)
Step 8	Made a list	*Into Action* (p.76, paragraph 3)
Step 9	Made amends	*Into Action* (p.76-84)
Step 10	Continued personal inventory	*Into Action* (p. 84-85)
Step 11	Sought through prayer and meditation	*Into Action* (p. 86-88)
Step 12, Part 1	Tried to carry this message	*Working With Others* (p. 89-96)
Step 12, Part 2	Practice these principles	*Working With Others* (p. 96-103)

If you are talking about the problem, you cannot be talking about the solution.

"We of Alcoholic Anonymous are over one-hundred men and women who have removed from a seemingly hopeless condition of mind and body. To show other alcoholics precisely how we have recovered is the main purpose of this book. For them, we hope these pages will prove so convincing that no further authentication will be necessary."-Forward To First Edition (1939)

Big Book Step Study (BBSS) is an approach to working the Twelve Steps as laid out in the Big Book (Alcoholics Anonymous). There are over 100 BBSS Format Groups meeting seven days a week all across the country. BBSS meeting is both live and on zoom. A meeting list, and other information regarding the BBSS format, are available at https://bbstepstudy.org.

Butterflies and Paratroopers Are Not Born With Wings

"You gotta buy it, It's a riot."

This is not a regurgitated recovery book. First, it's funny. Second, it's one-of-a-kind. And third, it's not a self-help book. It's an operator's manual. It trains alcoholics, drug addicts, overeaters, codependents, and whatever else has an addictive personality with a smidge of OCD or dusting of ADHD how to operate the most complex, prone to breakdown, out-of-warranty piece of equipment ever made—that's you.

In 1989, one in ten in recovery were women. Thirty-three years hence, it's one in three. Milo's sobriety date is April Fool's Day, 1989. He asked a woman out on a date, and some guy took him to an AA meeting. So, if you don't think God has a sense of humor, you'd be wrong.

Butterflies and Paratroopers is written from the perspective of a retired Army paratrooper and air traffic controller. The author 'was there' when women first entered these male only occupations. He knows a woman warrior when he sees one.

With an iron fist in a velvet glove, the persona of a First Sergeant trains a butterfly to be a paratrooper. *"We used to think one way, and now we think another."* Developing a new philosophy requires clarity of thought. And the clarity of thought comes from knowing who you are? Why you are like that? And why it's important to change?

Using amusing "girl-snippets", and "recovery war stories", Milo connects real-life trials and tribulations with spirituality, sobriety, sanity, and serenity. You'll quickly see the similarities between twelve-step recovery programs and the army. They take anybody and have a wrench to fit every nut that walks through the door.

Brevity, clarity, simplicity is the mantra. If you're talking about the problem, you can't be working on the solution. B&P is written so you can open it anywhere, start reading, and find solutions. With wit and cynicism, Milo reworks the army's doctrine of *BE, KNOW, DO: Train to Win in a Complex World* to describe a program of action, design for living, and process of recovery that seems to work with people like us. And who are people like us? We are the ones who have tried everything else.

Be you alcoholic, drug addict, codependent, overeater or whatever, this book will not only solve that problem; it will provide a blueprint to be happy, joyous, and free.

If you are ready; the time is right. Put your jump boots on ladies, you're going to Jump School.

About the Author

Milo Martin is a retired Army First Sergeant with more than thirty-three years of continuous sobriety. He received a Master's Degree in Public Administration from the University of New Hampshire and a Certificate of Graduate Studies from Harvard. A former paratrooper, air traffic controller, and auxiliary nuclear reactor operator, he was "in the room" when women first broke into these traditionally male roles. While serving in the army, he completed the Addiction Counselor Education Program at Boston University, and, besides being a First Sergeant, served as substance abuse and suicide prevention NCO. Now as a tired, old, bald, grumpy, and dumpy white guy, he shuffles between New Hampshire and Texas going to meetings with his Irish Setter, Madaline.

Answers

Page 2
1. the landing.
2. get you on your feet
3. first round
4. life-and-death errand
5. True
6. True
7. That we forgive others
8. False
9. we begin
10. True
11. worst items in stock.
12. spiritually
13. We may not overcome drinking

Page 4
1. that's alcoholism
2. True
3. False
4. complete the seventh step.
5. diagnosis.
6. False
7. True
8. repetitive and trivial
9. admission; absolution.
10. All the above
11. pocketing pride and overcoming fear
12. truth out of you.
13. True

Page 6
1. Sunlight
2. Sunlight of the Spirit.
3. odorous influent
4. flushing the toilet.
5. When people know you are right
6. True
7. Because we lie to ourselves
8. From wrongs to defects
9. Telling the truth
10. Holding on to "worst items in stock"
11. pride, fear, nothing.
12. All the above

Page 8
1. All the above
2. Freedom from bondage of self
3. Beginning; demarcation
4. defenses.
5. False
6. detour, dead end, and one-way streets.
7. False
8. saint.
9. Halo; start over.
10. paragraph.

Page 10
1. The three questions in Step Six are?
    - "If we can answer to our satisfaction."
    - "Are you ready?"
    - "Can He?"
2. we ask (pray) for help.
3. reaffirmation and validation
4. "My Creator."
5. pride; shame.
6. Touchdowns
7. Fumbled; penalty
8. Drink; drink.
9. False
10. True
11. scythed down.
12. Marvel in God's grace
13. God's grace

Page 12
1. False
2. False
3. Brief, clear, and simple; sorrow
4. What can we do with negative thoughts
    - You can hold on to them and believe the lies you tell yourself.
    - You can drift into worry, remorse, and morbid reflection.
    - You can go to God at once, talk to someone immediately, make necessary amends quickly, and rapidly turn your thoughts to what is good in your life.
5. "thy will be done"
6. All the above
7. spirituality, sobriety, sanity and serenity
8. True
9. stones; God

Page 14
1. Mirrored
2. sad sight indeed.
3. Weaker; heavier, astonishing difficult to solve.
4. A drink
5. being found out.
6. negative thoughts
7. moment.
8. True
9. brief, clear and simple.
10. Diligence, devotion and discipline
11. strength and the sanity
12. power of God.

Page 16
1. esteem
2. 8 billion people on the planet
3. all your ability.
4. knocked down.
5. contempt
6. Achievable; impossible
7. True
8. think; thinking.
9. True
10. development,

Page 18
1. To receive more of the same.
2. ceremony, training, anointment.
3. True
4. Ordinary; extraordinary
5. deflation.
6. defeat.
7. Step Ten and Eleven.
8. True
9. Show up after the humiliation.
10. "thy will be done"
11. To remind you God is there for you.

Page 20
1. regret it, then forget it.
2. True
3. True
4. Business
5. Selfishness; humility
6. True
7. False
8. Hostage
9. Religion
10. We give Him all the pieces.
11. ready; willing; right

Page 22
1. deflate the ego.
2. witness.
3. Those tormenting ghosts of yesterday we'd rather not remember.
4. pride and fear
5. Reluctant
6. We still carry our character defects with us.
7. spiritual growth
8. All of the above
9. True
10. burden we carry.
11. fearless admission; defects
12. We get rid of isolation.
13. terrified and lonely.

Page 24
1. understood.
2. We had to talk to somebody
3. True
4. forgiveness
5. deficiencies
6. experience with humility.
7. True
8. great and small
9. even know we have.
10. dangerous.
11. honest
12. right our wrongs with amends

Page 26
1. intentions and motivations
2. Camouflage
3. they are doing God will.
4. discussing matters with others
5. whom this will be.
6. virtue
7. intimate confidant
8. indescribable relief
9. There is a sense of humility and serenity.
10. forgiveness.

Page 28
1. spiritually
2. begin
3. Clarity of thought comes from knowing.
   - What we are like,
   - Why we are like that, and
   - Why it's important to change
4. bondage of self
5. human power can cure alcoholism
6. clean house; the three pertinent ideas
7. miracle of healing
8. commit suicide; installment plan
9. They believe the next time will be different.
10. Alcoholic; alcoholic
11. grace of God
12. We used to think one way and now we think another.

Page 30
1. obtainable objectives.
2. True
3. "No, I can't give this up yet."
4. God gave us self-will.
5. To be assured He will hear from us.
6. oppose; shun
7. self-preservation; punishment
8. exalt in our defects
9. Criticizing; self-righteousness
10. When it comes to … we alcoholics are masters of procrastination.
    - the leveling of our pride,
    - confession of shortcoming, and
    - implementing a spiritual solution,

Page 32
1. progress not perfection.
2. One seeks self-centered objectives and the other perfection.
3. False
4. True
5. Our worst items in stock.
6. One
7. Progress
8. life; thinking
9. open-mindedness
10. unconstitutionally willing
11. False
12. What questions do we ask in step six?
    - Have we answered to our satisfaction?
    - Are we now ready?
    - Can He take our defects away?

Page 34
1. Humility
2. Sober
3. We can't imagine life either with or without alcohol.
4. True
5. False
6. mess of things
7. Oblivion; what we want.
8. Humility; honesty
9. Lack of values
10. happiness
11. A desire to do God's will.
12. successive humiliating defeats
13. first step

Page 36
1. necessity
2. selfishness and self-centeredness
3. True
4. True
5. It disturbs our equilibrium
6. clarity of thought
7. All the above
8. revolutionary change
9. True
10. learn; learn.
11. antidote
12. False
13. Shortcomings

Page 38
1. Assurance God can do for us, what we cannot do for ourselves.
2. All the above
3. False
4. defects of character
5. better do His will.
6. thoughts, words, deeds, and actions
7. sanity with humility.
8. God; peace of mind
9. source of our trouble is
10. which is the way we think; which is the way we act,
11. The deal we made with God in Step Three.

Made in United States
Troutdale, OR
07/20/2023